Learning about Cats

THE RAGDOLL CAT

by Joanne Mattern

Consultant:
Judy Kay Halsey
CFA Ragdoll Breed Council Secretary
CFA Ragdolls of America Group Secretary
Cat Purebred Rescue
Ragmuff's Ragdolls, Kirkland, Washington

CAPSTONE
HIGH-INTEREST
BOOKS

an imprint of Capstone Press

Capstone High-Interest Books are published by Capstone Press
151 Good Counsel Drive, P.O. Box 669, Mankato, Minnesota 56002
http://www.capstone-press.com

Library of Congress Cataloging-in-Publication Data
Mattern, Joanne, 1963–
The Ragdoll cat/by Joanne Mattern.
    p.cm.—(Learning about cats)
    Includes bibliographical references and index (p. 48).
    ISBN 0-7368-0897-3
    1. Ragdoll cat—Juvenile literature. [1. Ragdoll cat. 2. Cats. 3. Pets.] I. Title.
II. Series.
SF449.R34 M38 2002
636.8'3—dc21   00-013072

Summary: Discusses the history, development, habits, and care of Ragdoll cats.

Editorial Credits
Leah K. Pockrandt, editor; Lois Wallentine, product planning editor; Linda Clavel,
    cover designer and illustrator; Katy Kudela, photo researcher

Photo Credits
Jim Brown, cover, 6, 10, 15, 16, 19, 22, 24, 38, 40–41
Joan Balzarini, 27
Nancy M. McCallum, 4, 9, 13, 20, 28, 31, 32, 35, 37

**Special thanks to Kristie Long of Longfellow Cattery, Olympia, Washington,
for her assistance with this book.**

1 2 3 4 5 6 07 06 05 04 03 02

Table of Contents

Quick Facts about the Ragdoll

Description

Size: Ragdoll cats have broad, heavy-boned, and muscular bodies. They are medium-sized to large-sized cats.

Weight: Male Ragdolls weigh between 14 and 18 pounds (6.4 and 8.2 kilograms). Females are slightly smaller. They weigh between 8 and 12 pounds (3.6 and 5.4 kilograms).

Physical features: Ragdolls have large, heavy bodies. Their soft fur is medium to long in length. They have broad, wedge-shaped heads. Their large, oval eyes are always blue.

Color: Ragdoll cats can be one of eight colors. Ragdolls' coats also can have different patterns. Ragdolls have light-colored coats. The fur on their ears, face, legs, and tail is darker than their coats. These dark areas of fur are called points.

Development
Place of origin: Ragdoll cats originated in California.

History of breed: Ann Baker developed the Ragdoll breed in the early 1960s. She bred a white female longhaired cat to a male longhaired cat. It is believed that the resulting kittens were bred to other cats with Siamese markings.

Numbers: In 2000, the Cat Fanciers' Association (CFA) registered 547 Ragdolls. Owners who register their Ragdolls register the cats' breeding records with an official organization. The CFA is the world's largest organization of cat breeders. But The International Cat Association (TICA) registers more Ragdolls than the CFA. In 2000, TICA registered 2,826 Ragdolls.

Chapter 1
The Ragdoll Cat

The Ragdoll cat is quiet, gentle, and affectionate. Many people value the breed's long, soft fur. The Ragdoll's calm personality makes it popular with people who want a gentle companion.

Appearance

Most Ragdolls are large-sized cats. The breed is one of the largest domestic cat breeds. Ragdolls can weigh 20 pounds (9.1 kilograms) or more. Male Ragdolls usually weigh between 14 and 18 pounds (6.4 and 8.2 kilograms). Females are slightly smaller. Females usually weigh between 8 and 12 pounds (3.6 and 5.4 kilograms). Ragdolls have wide, sturdy, and muscular bodies. It may take up to four years for Ragdolls to reach their full size.

Ragdolls are large, friendly cats.

Ragdolls have a double coat. They have a thin layer of plush fur near the skin. This undercoat is covered by a layer of lightweight, long, silky fur. The Ragdoll's fur does not easily clump together in mats like the coats of other longhaired breeds.

Ragdolls may be a variety of colors and patterns. All Ragdoll cats have points. These dark areas of fur are on the cats' ears, face, tail, and legs. Ragdoll kittens are born white. The points begin to appear when the kittens are a few days old. Ragdoll cats' permanent coat color patterns and points develop by the time they are 4 years old. The color gets darker as the cat gets older.

Personality

Ragdolls are playful and friendly cats. They seem to enjoy being around people and other animals. Ragdolls often follow people around and want to share in their activities.

Ragdolls seem to enjoy being held. When picked up, some Ragdolls go limp. This behavior resembles picking up a rag doll toy. Ragdolls received their name because of this behavior.

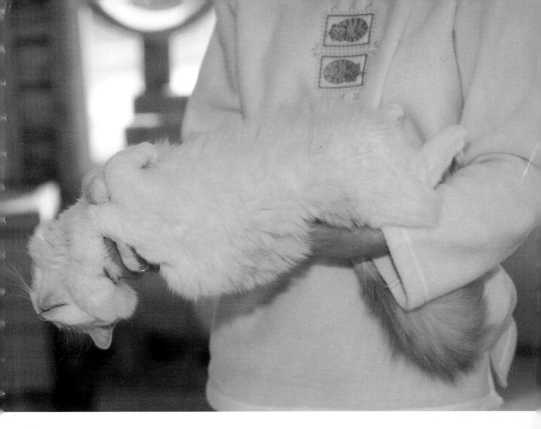

Some Ragdoll cats go limp when held.

Ragdoll cats are quiet. They do not meow much. They seem to enjoy quietly watching the people and animals around them.

Ragdolls make good pets for families. The breed does not demand constant attention. Ragdolls seem to be easygoing. They also get along well with dogs and other cats.

Chapter 2

Development of the Breed

The Ragdoll is one of the newest cat breeds. It was developed in the 1960s in California.

A Strange Story

A myth exists about the origin of Ragdolls. This false story says that the breed was created after a car accidentally struck a pregnant longhaired white cat. The cat's brain was damaged as a result of the accident. This injury changed the cat's personality. The cat became extremely quiet and gentle. Following the accident, the cat's body also went limp when held. The cat later gave birth to her kittens. These kittens were born with the same limp body and gentle personality as their mother.

The Ragdoll breed has a mysterious origin.

People now know this story is not true. A cat's personality and physical condition can change as a result of an accident. But it is impossible for these changes to be passed to the cat's offspring. An accident cannot change a cat's physical makeup.

The Truth about Ragdolls

A woman from California named Ann Baker developed the Ragdoll breed in the early 1960s. Baker crossed a longhaired white cat named Josephine to another longhaired cat. It is believed that both of these cats had markings similar to those of Siamese cats. The mating produced a mitted, seal-point male named Daddy Warbucks. This cat had a cream-colored coat with dark points. He also had white mitts on his four paws. Baker later crossed Josephine, Daddy Warbucks, and other longhaired cats.

It is not known what breeds Baker used to develop the Ragdoll. Some people believe that Baker used Persian, Birman, and Burmese cats. Other people think that Baker did not use purebred cats. They think she selected

Many people believe the first Ragdolls were mitted seal points.

longhaired cats with certain features for her breeding program.

The IRCA and the RFCI
In 1971, Baker founded the International Ragdoll Cat Association (IRCA). Baker had strict rules about how her Ragdolls should be

bred. But cat associations did not recognize IRCA Ragdolls. Owners could not enter these cats in cat shows.

Other breeders did not agree with the IRCA rules. Two of these breeders were Laura and Denny Dayton. The Daytons bought a pair of IRCA Ragdolls. They decided to develop the breed so that other cat associations would accept it.

The Daytons worked to create a standardized breeding program for Ragdoll cats. In 1975, the Ragdoll Fanciers Club International (RFCI) was formed. The RFCI publicized the breed.

The IRCA still exists. But IRCA Ragdolls are not accepted by any other cat organizations. All cat associations in North America accept Ragdolls. These associations include the Cat Fanciers' Association (CFA) and The International Cat Association (TICA).

The RFCI helped increase the popularity of Ragdolls.

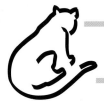

Chapter 3

Today's Ragdoll

Ragdolls are known for their appearance, friendliness, and calm nature. They have earned the nickname "the gentle giants."

Points, Colors, and Patterns

Ragdoll cats' coats can be several patterns and colors. The breed's colors are seal, blue, chocolate, lilac, red, cream, cinnamon, and fawn. Seal is dark brown. The blue color on Ragdolls is blue-gray. The chocolate color is light brown. The lilac color is pink-gray. The red color is red-orange. The cream ranges from dark off-white to very light brown. The cinnamon color is red-brown. The fawn color is light yellow-brown.

All Ragdoll cats have points. These dark areas of fur often are located on Ragdolls' ears, tail, face, and legs. The rest of Ragdolls' bodies are lighter in color. For example, seal-point Ragdolls

Ragdolls may have one of several colors and patterns.

have cream-colored coats with dark brown points. Ragdolls that have no color pattern other than points are called colorpoints. A colorpoint Ragdoll's coat has no white fur.

Ragdolls have a special gene that causes them to have points. Genes are parts of cells that are passed from parents to their offspring. Genes determine how the offspring will look. The point gene is a recessive gene. Ragdolls with this gene do not always produce kittens that look like them.

The point gene in Ragdolls is heat sensitive. Cool parts of the Ragdoll body have dark fur. These parts include the face, paws, tail, and ears. Warm parts of the body have lighter fur.

All animals with this heat-sensitive gene are born with white coats. Points begin to appear when a kitten is a few days old. Points become darker as the cat grows older. Fur on other parts of the body also may turn darker as the cat grows older. Blood does not circulate as well in older animals. Parts of their bodies become cooler with age.

Ragdolls may have solid points, lynx points, or tortie points. Ragdolls with lynx points have lightly striped coats and heavily striped points.

Ragdoll kittens may not look like their parents.

Tortie-point or tortoiseshell-point Ragdolls have points that resemble tortoise shells. This pattern consists of patches of black, red, and cream.

Other Patterns
Some Ragdolls are mitted. Like colorpoints, these cats have dark points and light-colored bodies. But a mitted Ragdoll has white mitts on its front paws and white "boots" on its back legs and feet. A mitted Ragdoll also has a white stripe on its stomach, a white chin, and a white chest.

Some Ragdolls have tufts of fur between their toes.

Bi-color Ragdoll cats have dark points on their ears, tail, and the outer part of their face. All four legs, their underbody, chest, and an upside-down "V" marking on their face are white. A Ragdoll also may have white splotches on its back. The darker color covers the cat's back and extends almost to its stomach.

Van Ragdolls are mostly white. They have dark markings on their ears, tail, and the top area of their face. They also may have a couple of dark markings on their body.

Breed Standard

Judges look for certain physical features when they judge Ragdolls in cat shows. These features are called the breed standard.

The breed standard says that a Ragdoll cat should have a long, broad body. Its legs should be heavy and of medium length. Its paws should be large and round. It may have tufts of fur between its toes.

A Ragdoll's fur should be long, thick, and soft. Ragdoll point colors must be seal, chocolate, blue, lilac, red, or cream. The CFA accepts bi-color and van Ragdolls in these six colors for championship status. This status is the highest level of competition at a cat show. Other major cat associations accept bi-color, mitted, and colorpoint Ragdolls in eight colors. The colors are seal, blue, chocolate, lilac, red, cream, cinnamon, and fawn. A Ragdoll should have a ruff of longer fur around its neck. Its tail should be full and long.

A Ragdoll cat's head should be wide and shaped like a wedge. This shape looks like an upside-down triangle. Its ears should be wide at the base and rounded at the top. The ears also should tip forward. A Ragdoll must have blue, oval-shaped eyes.

Chapter 4

Owning a Ragdoll

People can adopt Ragdolls in several ways. They may buy Ragdolls from breeders. People also may adopt Ragdolls from animal shelters or rescue organizations. Ragdolls from breeders can cost several hundred dollars. It often costs much less to adopt Ragdoll cats from animal shelters or breed rescue organizations.

Ragdoll Breeders

People can buy show-quality and good pet-quality Ragdoll cats from good breeders. These people carefully breed their cats to make sure that they are healthy and meet the breed standard. Breeders usually own both parents of the kittens that they sell. People then can see how the kitten will look as an adult.

People can meet a breeder's cats before they buy a Ragdoll kitten.

Good breeders sell show-quality and good pet-quality Ragdoll adult cats and kittens.

Many Ragdoll cat breeders live in the United States and Canada. People can find local breeders at cat shows. People can talk to the breeders and see their cats at the shows.

Breeders also advertise in newspapers and magazines. These ads are organized by breed. Ads include the names, addresses, and phone numbers of breeders. Some breeders also have Internet sites. People should get the medical histories of the breeders' cats before they buy a cat from the breeders. They also should check the breeders' references. People should contact others who have bought cats from the breeders. These owners can provide information about their experiences with the breeders.

Animal Shelters
Many people adopt cats from animal shelters. These places keep unwanted animals and try to find homes for them.

An animal shelter can be a good place to adopt a cat for several reasons. Many more animals are brought to shelters than there are people available to adopt them. Animals that are not adopted often are euthanized. Shelter workers euthanize animals by injecting them with substances that stop their breathing or heartbeat. Animal shelters also offer less expensive pets. Most shelters charge only a small fee. Some veterinarians may provide discounts on medical services for shelter animals.

Shelters do have some disadvantages. Shelters often have mixed-breed pets available for adoption instead of purebred cats such as the Ragdoll. People interested in adopting a Ragdoll cat can ask shelter workers to contact them if a Ragdoll is brought to the shelter.

Another problem with shelter cats is that their histories often are unknown. Shelter workers may not know anything about the cats' parents, health, or behavior. Some of these cats may have medical or behavioral problems.

Despite these problems, many good pets are available at animal shelters. Adopting from a shelter is a good choice for people who do not plan to breed or show their Ragdoll cats. Shelter animals usually do not have papers showing that they are registered with an official cat club. Cats without registration papers can compete only in the household pet group in cat shows.

Breed Rescue Organizations

People interested in adopting purebred Ragdoll cats may want to contact breed rescue organizations. Organization members find unwanted or neglected animals. They care for the animals and try to find owners to adopt them.

Breed rescue organizations are similar to animal shelters in many ways. But most organizations rescue only certain breeds of cats or dogs. They rarely euthanize the animals. Breed rescue organizations keep Ragdoll cats until people are available to adopt them.

People can find excellent pets through shelters and breed rescue organizations.

Breed rescue organizations charge less than breeders do. People may find purebred Ragdolls for a small fee. These cats even may be registered.

People can find information about Ragdoll rescue organizations in several ways. These organizations often have their own Internet sites. They may advertise in magazines or newspapers. Animal shelters also may refer people to Ragdoll breed rescue organizations.

Chapter 5

Caring for a Ragdoll

Ragdolls are strong, healthy cats. With proper care, owners can have a healthy companion for many years. Ragdolls can live 15 years or more.

Indoor and Outdoor Cats

Some cat owners allow their cats to roam outdoors. This practice is not safe. Cats that roam outdoors have a much greater risk of developing diseases than indoor cats. Outdoor cats also face dangers from other animals and cars.

It is especially important to keep Ragdoll cats inside. Ragdolls have a calm nature. They often do not fight back if another animal attacks them. Indoor Ragdolls are safe from cats, dogs, or other animals that may harm them.

Owners of indoor cats need to provide their cats with a litter box. Owners fill the box with small bits of clay called litter. Cats eliminate

Ragdolls need scratching posts.

waste in litter boxes. Owners should clean
the waste out of the box each day. They should
change the litter often. Cats are clean animals.
They may refuse to use a dirty litter box.

Both indoor and outdoor cats need to scratch.
Cats mark their territories by leaving their scent
on objects that they scratch. Cats also scratch
to release tension and keep their claws sharp.
This habit can be a problem if cats scratch on
furniture, carpet, or curtains. Owners should
provide their cats with a scratching post. They
can buy scratching posts at pet stores. They also
may make scratching posts from wood and carpet.

Health Problems

Ragdoll cats have few health problems. The most
common problem is hairballs. Many longhaired
cats have hairballs at one time or another. Cats
often swallow fur when they groom their coats
with their tongues. This fur can form into a ball in
the cat's stomach. The cat then vomits the hairball.
Large hairballs can become lodged in the cat's
digestive system. A veterinarian then may have
to perform surgery to remove these hairballs.

Regular brushing is the best way to prevent
hairballs. Brushing removes loose fur before the
cat can swallow it. Owners also can give Ragdolls

Ragdolls often swallow fur when they groom their coats.

medicines to treat hairballs. These medicines contain petroleum jelly. The jelly coats the hairballs in the cat's stomach. The hairballs then pass harmlessly in the cat's waste.

Cats sometimes get diseases that are passed down from their parents. Good cat breeders test their animals for these diseases. They will not breed animals that suffer from serious illnesses. Breeders should have information on their cats' medical histories. This information is important when choosing a Ragdoll cat.

Some Ragdolls prefer to eat dry cat food.

Ragdoll Myths

Many myths exist about Ragdolls. Some of these
myths are about the Ragdoll's health or physical
features. Some people believe that Ragdolls
cannot feel pain. But Ragdolls do feel the same
amount of pain as other cat breeds.

Another myth is that Ragdolls have deformed
bones or muscles. Some people believe that this
physical feature is the reason Ragdolls' bodies
relax when held. Ragdolls do not have any physical

deformities. But veterinarians do not know why some Ragdoll cats relax their muscles.

Some people think the reason Ragdolls are calm is because the cats are not very smart. That idea is not true. Ragdolls are known to be quick learners. Some owners teach their Ragdolls tricks such as retrieving toys.

Feeding

Ragdoll cats need high-quality food. Some pet foods sold by supermarkets or pet stores provide a balanced, healthy diet.

Some owners feed their cats dry food. This food usually is less expensive than other types of food. Dry food can help keep cats' teeth clean. This type of food also will not spoil if it is left in a dish.

Other owners prefer to feed their cats moist, canned food. This type of food will spoil if it is left out for more than one hour. Owners who feed their cats moist food usually feed their adult cats twice each day. The amount of food needed depends on the individual cat.

Both types of food are suitable for Ragdoll cats. Different cats may prefer certain food. It is best to have dry food available at all times.

Owners then can give their cats canned food during the day.

Cats need to drink water to stay healthy. Owners should keep their cats' bowls filled with fresh, clean water. Owners should dump and refill the water bowls each day.

Grooming

A Ragdoll's fur is easy to groom. It does not mat or tangle as easily as the fur of other longhaired cat breeds. Owners need to brush their Ragdoll's coat once each week. A natural bristle brush works best. Plastic or other synthetic brushes often cause the cat's fur to stand on end from static electricity. Owners also can use a comb on thicker areas of the coat.

Owners should brush Ragdolls more often during spring. Ragdolls shed their winter coats at this time. Frequent brushings will help the cats get rid of loose hair.

Owners must be gentle when they brush or comb their Ragdoll cats. Owners can break off pieces of fur if they brush too hard. They also can scrape their cats' skin.

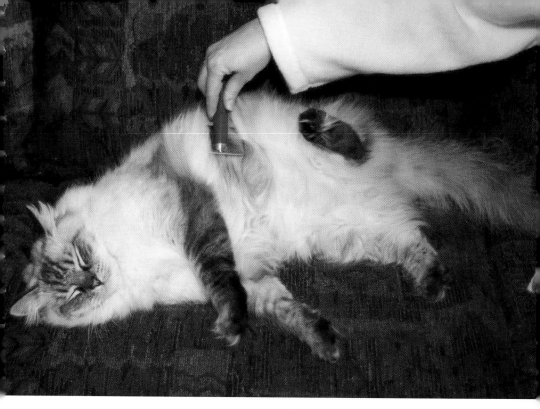

Owners need to brush or comb their Ragdolls once each week.

Nail Care

The tip of a cat's claw is called the nail. Ragdoll cats need their nails trimmed every few weeks. Trimming helps reduce damage if cats scratch carpet or furniture. It also protects cats from infections caused by ingrown nails. This condition causes the area around the claw to become red and swollen. Infections can occur when a cat does not sharpen its claws often. The claws then grow into the bottom of the paw.

Owners should first trim their Ragdolls' nails when the cats are young. The kittens will become used to having their nails trimmed as they grow older. Veterinarians can show owners how to trim their cats' nails with a special nail clipper.

Dental Care

Ragdoll cats also need regular dental care to protect their teeth and gums from plaque. This coating of bacteria and saliva causes tooth decay and gum disease. Owners should brush their cats' teeth at least once each week. They can use a special toothbrush made for cats or a soft cloth. They also should brush the cats' teeth with a toothpaste that is made for cats. Owners should never use toothpaste made for people. Cats become sick if they swallow it.

Brushing may not be enough to remove the plaque from older cats' teeth. They may need to have their teeth cleaned once each year by a veterinarian.

Veterinarian Visits

Ragdoll cats must visit a veterinarian regularly for checkups. Most veterinarians recommend

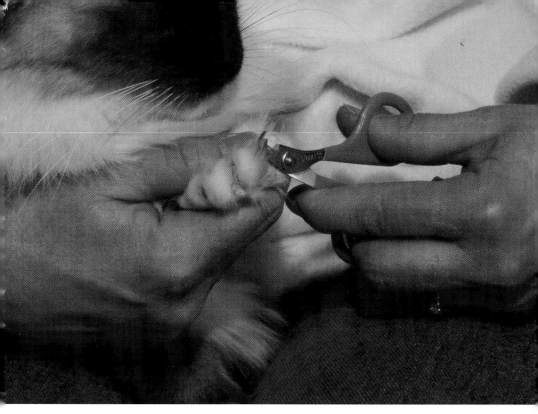

Owners can use a special nail clipper to clip their Ragdoll's nails.

yearly visits for cats. Older cats may need to visit a veterinarian more often. Cats tend to have more health problems as they age.

A new Ragdoll owner should take their cat to a veterinarian for a checkup as soon as possible. The veterinarian will check the cat's heart, lungs, internal organs, eyes, ears, mouth, and coat.

Ragdolls also need vaccinations. These shots of medicine help prevent serious diseases such as rabies and feline panleukopenia. Rabies is a

With proper care, healthy Ragdolls can live for 15 years or more.

deadly disease that is spread by animal bites. Most states and provinces have laws that require owners to vaccinate their cats against rabies. Feline panleukopenia also is called feline distemper. This disease causes fever, vomiting, and death. Veterinarians also can vaccinate Ragdolls against several respiratory diseases that cause breathing or lung problems.

Cats should receive some vaccinations each year. They need other vaccinations less often. Breeders and veterinarians have information on which vaccinations Ragdoll cats need. Owners should keep a record of their cats' vaccination dates. This record helps owners make sure that their cats have received all the needed vaccinations.

Veterinarians also spay female cats and neuter male cats. These surgeries prevent cats from breeding. Owners who do not plan to breed their cats should have them spayed or neutered. These surgeries keep unwanted kittens from being born. Spaying and neutering also help prevent diseases such as infections and cancers of the reproductive organs. Spayed and neutered cats usually have calmer personalities than cats that are not spayed or neutered. They also are less likely to wander away from home to find mates.

Regular grooming, a healthy diet, and proper veterinary care are important parts of caring for a Ragdoll. Owners who follow these guidelines can enjoy many years with their cats.

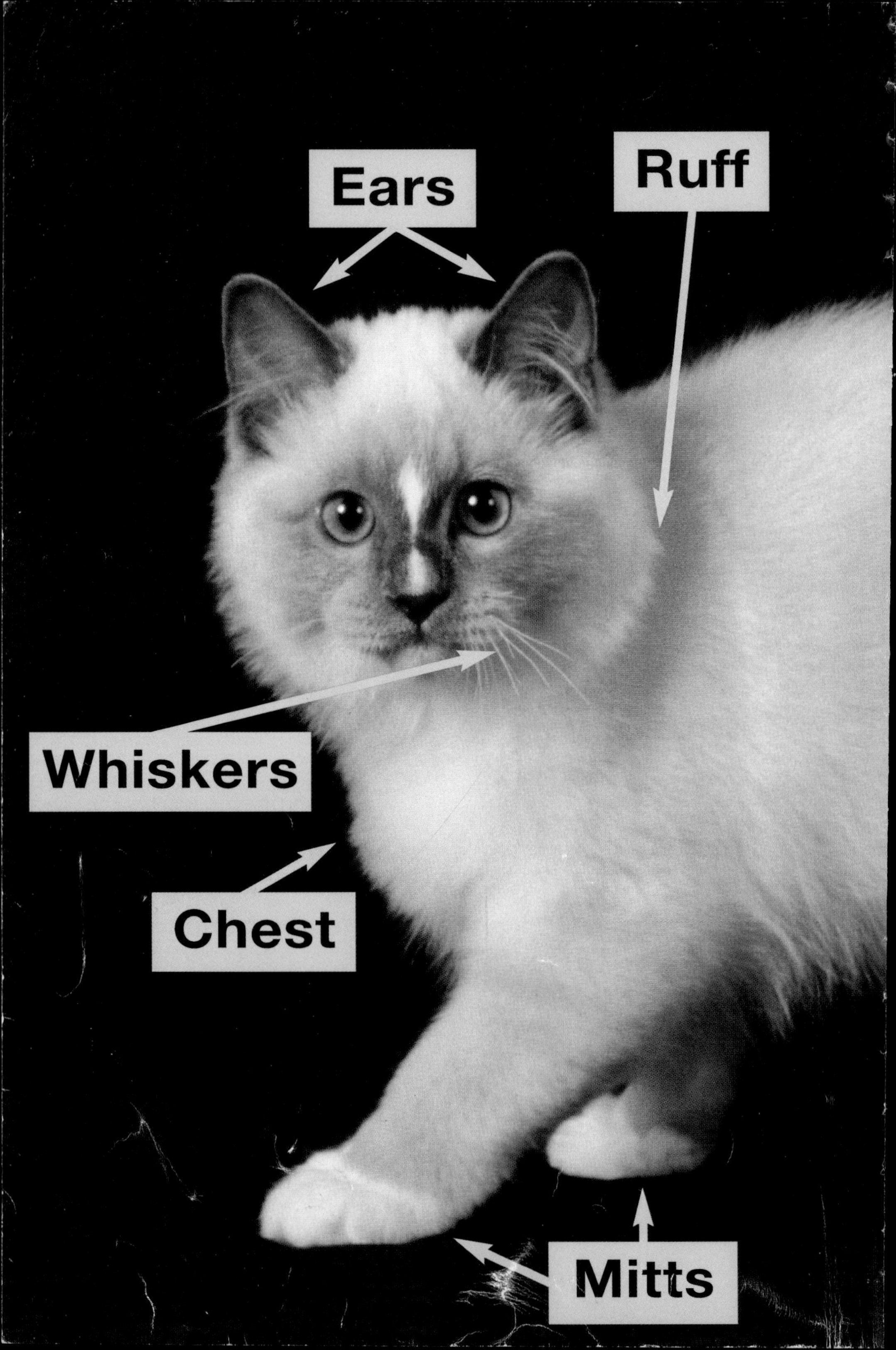
Ears
Ruff
Whiskers
Chest
Mitts

Tail

Hocks

Paws

Quick Facts about Cats

A male cat is called a tom. A female cat is called a queen. A young cat is called a kitten. A family of kittens born at one time is called a litter.

Origin: Shorthaired cat breeds descended from a type of African wildcat called *Felis lybica*. Longhaired breeds may have descended from Asian wildcats. People domesticated or tamed these breeds as early as 1500 B.C.

Types: The Cat Fanciers' Association accepts 40 domestic cat breeds for competition. The smallest breeds weigh about 5 to 7 pounds (2.3 to 3.2 kilograms) when grown. The largest breeds can weigh more than 18 pounds (8.2 kilograms). Cat breeds may be either shorthaired or longhaired. Cats' coats can be a variety of colors. These colors include many shades of white, black, gray, brown, and red.

Reproduction: Most cats are sexually mature at 5 or 6 months. A sexually mature female cat goes into estrus several times each year. Estrus also is called "heat." During this time, she can mate with a male. Kittens are born about 65 days after breeding. An average litter includes four kittens.

Development: Kittens are born blind and deaf. Their eyes open about 10 days after birth. Their hearing develops at the same time. They can live on their own when they are 6 weeks old.

Life span: With good care, cats can live 15 or more years.

Sight: A cat's eyesight is adapted for hunting. Cats are good judges of distance. They see movement more easily than detail. Cats also have excellent night vision.

Hearing: Cats can hear sounds that are too high for humans to hear. A cat can turn its ears to focus on different sounds.

Smell: A cat has an excellent sense of smell. Cats use scents to establish their territories. Cats scratch or rub the sides of their faces against objects. These actions release a scent from glands between their toes or in their skin.

Taste: Cats cannot taste as many foods as people can. For example, cats are not very sensitive to sweet tastes.

Touch: Cats' whiskers are sensitive to touch. Cats use their whiskers to touch objects and sense changes in their surroundings.

Balance: Cats have an excellent sense of balance. They use their tails to help keep their balance. Cats can walk on narrow objects without falling. They usually can right themselves and land on their feet during falls from short distances.

Communication: Cats use many sounds to communicate with people and other animals. They may meow when hungry or hiss when afraid. Cats also purr. Scientists do not know exactly what causes cats to make this sound. Cats often purr when they are relaxed. But they also may purr when they are sick or in pain.

Words to Know

breeder (BREED-ur)—someone who breeds and raises cats or other animals

breed standard (BREED STAN-durd)—certain physical features in a breed that judges look for at a cat show

estrus (ESS-truss)—a physical state of a female cat during which she will mate with a male cat; estrus also is known as "heat."

euthanize (YOO-thuh-nize)—to painlessly put an animal to death by injecting it with a substance that stops its breathing or heartbeat

neuter (NOO-tur)—to remove a male animal's testicles so that it cannot reproduce

points (POINTZ)—dark-colored areas of fur often found on Ragdoll cats' ears, faces, legs, and tails

spay (SPAY)—to remove a female animal's uterus and ovaries so that it cannot reproduce

vaccination (vak-suh-NAY-shun)—a shot of medicine that protects a person or animal from disease

To Learn More

Davis, Karen Leigh. *Ragdoll Cats: Everything about Purchase, Nutrition, Health Care, Grooming, Behavior, and Showing.* A Complete Pet Owner's Manual. Hauppauge, N.Y.: Barron's, 1999.

Petras, Kathryn, and Ross Petras. *Cats: 47 Favorite Breeds, Appearance, History, Personality, and Lore.* Fandex Family Field Guides. New York: Workman Publishing, 1997.

Strobel, Gary A., and Susan A. Nelson. *Guide to Owning a Ragdoll Cat.* Popular Cat Library. Philadelphia: Chelsea House, 1999.

Verhoef-Verhallen, Esther J.J. *The Cat Encyclopedia.* Buffalo, N.Y.: Firefly Books, 1997.

You can read articles about Ragdoll cats in *Cat Fancy* and *Cats* magazines.

Useful Addresses

Canadian Cat Association (CCA)
289 Rutherford Road South
Unit 18
Brampton, ON L6W 3R9
Canada

Cat Fanciers' Association (CFA)
P.O. Box 1005
Manasquan, NJ 08736-0805

The International Cat Association (TICA)
P.O. Box 2684
Harlingen, TX 78551

Ragdoll Fanciers Club International
1046 Moon Valley Road
Billings, MT 59105

Ragdoll International (RI)
103 Perry Drive
New Milford, CT 06776

Ragdolls of America Group (RAG)
P.O. Box 2324
Kirkland, WA 98083

Internet Sites

Canadian Cat Association (CCA)
http://www.cca-afc.com

Cat Fanciers' Association (CFA)
http://www.cfainc.org

The International Cat Association (TICA)
http://www.tica.org

The Ragdoll Connection Network
http://www.ragdoll-cats.com

Ragdoll Fanciers Club International
http://rfci.org

Ragdoll International (RI)
http://www.ragdollintl.com

Ragdolls of America Group (RAG)
http://ragofcfa.tripod.com

Index